I CANCEL YOU

A journey of faith, healing power
and authority, when you're
battling long-term illness

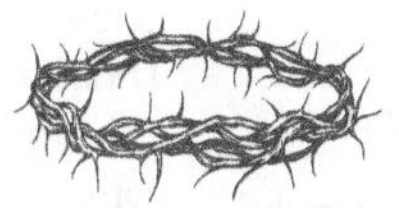

BY

CHONTAE TAINGAHUE

Wild Side Publishing
PO Box 33, Ruawai 0549
Northland, New Zealand
wildsidepublishing.com

Cataloguing in Publication Data:
Title: I Cancel You

ISBN: 978-0-473-45818-8 (pbk)
ISBN: 978-0-473-45819-5 (epub)
ISBN: 978-0-473-48109-4 (audiobook)

Subjects: New Zealand Non-Fiction, Autobiography, Christian Living, Mind Body Spirit, Inspirational, Coping with Life, Healing, Cancer.

First printing 2018 benefitz.co.nz
Second printing 2019 benefitz.co.nz
International listing 2018 Ingram Spark

DEDICATION

I dedicate this book to all those continuing to persevere for their miracle, enduring through all kinds of trials.

I also dedicate it to the family and friends who are standing beside their loved one as their Aaron and Hur, raising their arms to God when they can no longer do it themselves.

Lastly, this book is for my family. Without you, I could not have got through this. To my Hunk (husband), Aaron, and our children Iraia, Bianca, Nia, Ariana, Kepa, Hinenui-Te-Kaea and Anahera. I am blessed to have such a strong, supportive and loving family.

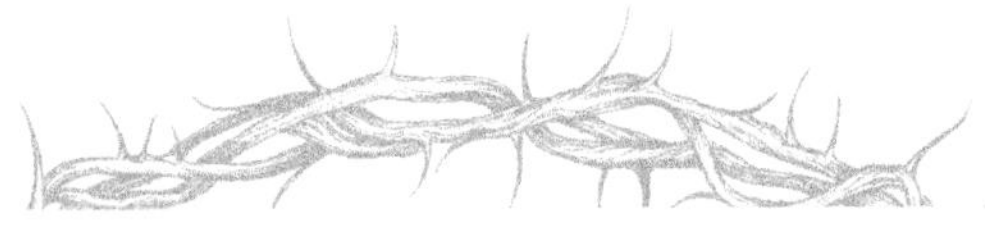

CONTENTS

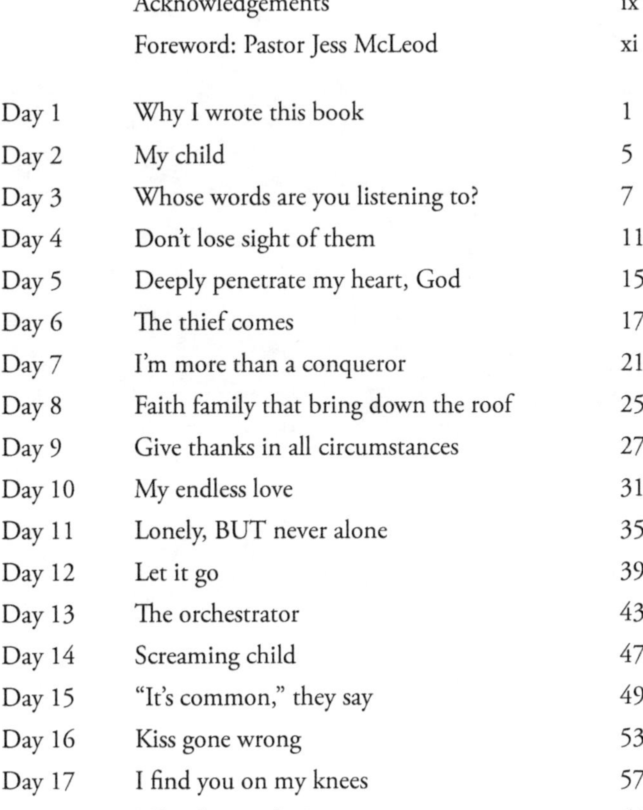

CONTENTS

ACKNOWLEDGEMENTS

I give all the glory to God, the author and finisher
of my faith, the almighty, powerful, Great I Am,
my provider, my healer, and above all,
my loving Father.

To my Lord and Saviour Jesus Christ: thank You for
Your selfless act of dying on the cross taking all our sins,
sickness, transgressions, iniquities and curses, and by
conquering death, making it possible for all of humanity
to be restored to God, giving us access to eternity.

To Holy Spirit: thank You for coming as the helper,
a guide, a nurturer, not to mention the
powerful gifts You bring us.

FOREWORD

I am a total believer in the healing power of Jesus. I have absolutely no doubt it is for today. Hebrews 13:8 says, **'He is the same yesterday, today and forever'**.

As a pastor, I often come across people in need of prayer because they have received bad news about their health. Sometimes I see or hear of miracle healings but for some it is not as wonderful or as simple as that as they go on a journey of recovery. This is why Chontae's account of her journey, told in simple everyday language, will be such an encourager. Chontae shares her highs and her lows, and what was required from her to gain victory in debilitating circumstance. I believe there are many keys here that will put the lies that can come to us to death, and bring light in the darkest of times.

Chontae shares how she came to a place of deeper trust in a loving, caring God, and received her healing. This book has been written with thought to the reader, in which keys and prayers have been included to give clear guidelines of what to do as you journey into full recovery.

Pastor Jess McLeod
House of Breakthrough, Gisborne

xii

DAY 1: THE BEGINNING

WHY I WROTE THIS BOOK

"Pancreatic cancer..." seemed to have a long-winded echo as the doctor spoke.

Maybe those weren't the words you or someone you love, received. Maybe the words echoed were a different form of cancer, terminal illness, or maybe like Apostle Paul, you have a long-standing thorn in your flesh causing you pain and suffering, even tormenting you. Whatever your reasons are, I wrote this book with you in mind.

Let me share my journey so you understand where I have come from and why I wrote this book. It was the year 2014, in the ninth month, on the 25th day. I was 34 years old, a wife to Aaron, whom I call 'the Hunk', and a devoted mum to our six children. I also helped lead and pastor our church with my Hunk.

As I waited in a room in the hospital, the doctor came in and spoke about the scans I had undergone over the last two days. He continued on speaking, saying there was a 99% chance I had pancreatic cancer.

I noticed everything in the room; how bland the colors looked. I thought they could do with some peaceful pictures, so when people received traumatic news, the room would be filled with love, peace and joy. The room suddenly felt smaller than when I first arrived and the ceiling was spinning. I felt my entire body freeze, I tried to breathe, but it seemed hard. I took a deep breath. Then, for some weird reason, after that long deep breath, I thought about the Christian Women's Conference, I was attending with 34 ladies from my church, in just two weeks time. I needed to go to this conference and couldn't see how, if I was to stay in the hospital. I doubted I would be well enough to make it to the conference if I had the surgery straight away. Then I heard the doctor say, "Do you have questions for me?"

The first question I asked was, "Can I go to my Christian women's conference in two weeks, and have the surgery after that?" The doctor replied, "Yes, I don't see why you can't. The lump in your pancreas is not going anywhere, I don't see it will cause much harm in these next two weeks."

Maybe you haven't experienced all the things I did that day, but you can relate to the chain of events and some shocking news from your own experience, the whirlwind of emotions and thoughts that came flying at you, leaving you numb. I wrote this book with you in mind, and many others who are going through a similar journey.

WHAT YOU WILL FIND IN THIS BOOK

The chapters are easy to read, and I've tried to keep them short. I wrote them for someone who has been persevering through a long-term illness. Believe me, the last thing, you want to do is read a book with long chapters.

There are 31 chapters, so you can read one each day of the month. The majority share part of my journey. This journey includes the victories, and the valleys. One moment we are high on the mountaintop, and the next—deep in the darkest valley. One thing you will notice is an everlasting love towards an imperfect human being, given by the main characters, Father God, Jesus, and Holy Spirit.

Some chapters have dates with either an excerpt from my diary, or a written summary of what happened on that day, bringing a personal touch to this book. It's like seeing the journey through my eyes.

At the end of every chapter is a short prayer, declaration or scripture for you to engage in. These have helped me in my most hopeless moments. They prepared me for the battle ahead, and showed how to appropriate the healing power of God to myself. They taught me to stand in my authority as a believer of Jesus Christ. ***Please, try not to skip these parts.*** There is power in the words we declare and decree with our mouth (Proverbs 18:21). These become our weapons of warfare. Like turning anxiety into gladness, (Proverbs 12:25), they propel us to experience everything that Jesus won for us, (Matthew 12:27) and much more. Take your time.

The last few chapters of this book talk about the power and authority we have as God's children through Jesus Christ. Day 31 contains a special healing prayer I wrote for you. It is a prayer that has helped me throughout my journey. I pray that the healing power of God will saturate you as you declare His Word and this prayer over your life today.

I'm looking forward to sharing my journey with you, and pray it will bless, encourage and uplift you—and that with each page you turn, you will encounter a living God.

DAY 2: MY CHILD

My child, pay attention to what I say. Listen carefully, to My words. Don't lose sight of them. Let them penetrate deep in your heart, for they bring life to those who find them, and healing to their whole body.

~Proverbs 4:20-22 NLT

Over the next few days, we will go deeper into this scripture. You'll also come across parts of my journey, and how I could overcome many struggles through activating this scripture in my life.

For today, read this scripture, then allow yourself to meditate on these words for a further five to ten minutes. Highlight words that stand out to you, and write them down in your journal. Take notes on why they stood out to you. What changes did you notice in your body, soul, and spirit? What words and promises has God given to you? Notice where He wants you to pay more attention.

At the end of this book, there is a chapter on five steps to going deeper with God. It is a guideline to going deeper into God's Word. This process is what I use today, and it has helped me uncover many mysteries in God's holy scriptures.

PRAYER

Father, I ask through Holy Spirit to illuminate Your words through the Word, the holy scriptures of Your Bible. Allow it to penetrate deeply into my heart.

In the mighty name of Jesus,

Amen

DAY 3: WHOSE WORDS ARE YOU LISTENING TO?

My child, pay attention to what I say.
Listen carefully, to My words.

~Proverbs 4:20 NLT

26 SEPTEMBER, 2014: PART 1 OF 3

I had many visitors throughout the day—believers, and non-believers, of my family and friends.

I listened to the many words across my dinner table. What about funeral insurance, and did I have a will? There were stories of people my family and friends knew, ones who had this cancer, and died not long after diagnosis. Others gave me facts they found online. For instance, they told me that there was a 3% chance of survival, and that was *after* chemo. Someone else also mentioned, if you were in surgery for over three hours; it meant there was hope, but if you're back in an hour—there was nothing the doctors could do.

All these words flying at me unsettled my spirit. *Who wouldn't be unsettled?* That's a lot to take in. I knew my family and friends loved me and meant well. They also had to come to grips with the news, and everyone responds differently. We must be gracious to those that do not know Jesus as their Lord and Saviour as yet. As believers and followers of Jesus, we are representatives of the Kingdom of Heaven, formed in the image of the Father, Son, and Holy Spirit. The way we treat others could be the tipping point for their salvation.

I made many agreements with God that day, and when I veer off course, the Holy Spirit reminds me to not allow negative influences hinder me, and not to agree with Satan's plans. I'm grateful for God's grace and mercy upon my life, and His faithfulness towards me, which reaches to the skies. He wouldn't leave me in the most vulnerable, downtrodden days during my journey. This is a promise to us all.

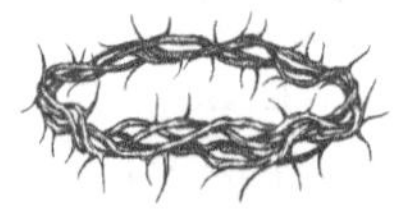

Here is one agreement I made:

PRAYER

God, I am your daughter, and I want to hear what You say, because Your words are the only truth that brings life. Holy Spirit, I need Your help to hear only God's words for my life. I cannot do it on my own.

Jesus, anything that does not line up with the Word of God, remove it from my ear gates. Any words I have made in agreement with pancreatic cancer, Jesus, I cancel them, and the assignment of death associated with them. I break their power in the name of Jesus.

Please come and wash my ear gates with Your blood that declares, I am healed and set free.

In the mighty name of Jesus,

Amen

HERE IS A TIP

Using an audio Bible was the best thing I did throughout my journey. It read the Bible to me when I couldn't, or I had no one to read it to me. I still use it today.

DAY 4:
DON'T LOSE SIGHT OF THEM

Not only would I hear many words spoken on this day, but the hospital presented lots of information, such as the five page information sheet on pancreatic cancer, given as a guide by my doctor. A friend wrote a note. I was expecting a note of encouragement, filled with God's Word; but instead, it was notes they found online about the cancer I might have. God bless my friend for wanting to ensure I was well informed!

Let me share a few more agreements I made with God, my eyes, and things I spoke to my family and friends about. This was to make sure the only word I would see and agree with, was the written Word of God—and I needed my family and friends to understand this. Here is an example I wrote to myself that day:

I'm a daughter of the most high God, and Jesus lives to intercede for me always. *I am in the 3% that will survive this cancer, and that's without chemo*—because Jesus lives in the 3%. He is the tipping point.

Here is what I asked of my close family and friends about a week before my surgery: I requested that the only word I wanted to hear, or see, was the Word of God—and what it said for my life.

"If you visit me in hospital, please understand that the Bible means so much, I would love you to read it to me. Please refrain from using negative words around me regarding my life, because I know that I will live. I do not agree with the diagnosis."

All my family and friends I spoke to, agreed to help me. When times get tough, write God's promises or words where you can see them; in a journal, diary, or put them down on paper, laminate it—and stick on the fridge, toilet door or in the kitchen. Anywhere you can see it! If you're struggling, call upon Holy Spirit to lead you back to Jesus and the agreements you made. I did this, and it worked.

It's important to remember there is no condemnation in Christ Jesus to those who love Him, because He has set you and I free. When you go through long-term illness, I understand the struggle can be real. Remember, Jesus is not counting how much you read His Word, prayed or didn't keep to your agreement. He understands, and has felt the pain you are going through; the trials and tribulations you will encounter on this journey. These agreements I made were to keep me focused on God's Kingdom, His truth and the love He had towards me. I put boundaries in place because I knew I had to pay attention to God's will for my life in this circumstance. His will is always for our good. There will be many things to distract you, hoping to make you a slave to the things of this world.

What are agreements you can make with God? They don't have to be long; just simple. Write them down in your journal.

PRAYER

> *Father God, I submit my eyes to you. I only want to see Your truth. Anything I have read or seen in the natural that does not bring life, **I cancel it** in the name of Jesus, and ask You, Jesus, to wash my eyes clean. Holy Spirit, help me see only through the eyes of the Lord.*
>
> *In the mighty name of Jesus,*
>
> *Amen*

DAY 5: DEEPLY PENETRATE
MY HEART, GOD

27 SEPTEMBER, 2014: AN EXCERPT FROM MY DIARY

PRAYER FOR TODAY

Lord, I need You more than ever. I'm scared for what lies ahead of me. I know You know the plans You have for my life, and they are for my good, and will prosper me. No harm will come against me. If it does, it will flee from me because I am Your daughter and You are my God above ALL gods.

Lord, I need Your Word because it is sharper than any double-edged sword, penetrates even to dividing soul and spirit, bone and marrow. It even judges the thoughts and attitudes deep in my heart. I give You permission to continue to deeply penetrate my heart. Search me, O Lord.

Lord, Your Word is like living water; it brings life like a deer pants for water. It is like a fire that burns everything up that does not align with Your truth. Burn the negative words I have allowed to settle in my heart and mind, the words I have heard or seen that are not true words, and that have assignments of death attached to them and come against me. I cancel those words, and come out of agreement—known or unknown to me. I break the power they may have over me in Jesus' mighty name.

You, O Lord, are the GREAT I AM; almighty, powerful, whose words never return void, for they are greater than Your name. They speak of life and bring healing into my body.

*Thank You that the words You speak are alive in me. For greater are they in me, than the words of this world could ever be. I will live to see the coming generations, because I have decided I will live, and not die, from this thing they call, 'pancreatic cancer.' **I cancel you, cancer, in Jesus' name.***

In the mighty name of Jesus,

Amen

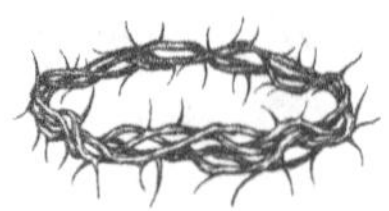

DAY 6: THE THIEF COMES

NINE MONTHS BEFORE MY VISIT
TO THE HOSPITAL

Hunk and I decided we would take the children and go to Wait-arere Beach, New Zealand. It was in the middle of January and the kids were still on school holidays. After some of the events that took place in 2013, we needed a fresh start to the new year, and we needed well-deserved family time.

It was during this time I felt ill and ended up in bed for most the time. Not your ideal way to spend your family holiday!

On one of the worst days I had, I remember hearing a voice while I slept:

"You're going to die... you're going to die... you're going to die..."

I heard those words repeated three times before they faded into the distance. I shivered for a moment, as I knew this voice. It was the voice of the thief, my foe and enemy of God—Satan!

I prayed: *"Lord Your Word says, Your sheep know Your voice.*

I know Your voice Lord, so I rebuke this voice that says I will die. Thief, I bind your words and cast them back where they came from. God, You say You gave me life through Your son, Jesus Christ. Amen."

I had little strength and kept my prayer short before falling asleep. The next morning, I felt much better.

Over the next nine months until my visit to the hospital, I would hear the same words: ***"You're going to die…"*** I would rebuke them in the name of Jesus.

When I received the news of pancreatic cancer, the words changed: ***"I told you, you will die…"***

A thief comes only to steal, kill and destroy. John 10:10a ESV

In times like this, we need the Word to penetrate deeply into our heart, our mind, body, soul and spirit. In the next part of this scripture, Jesus says:

"But I came to give life—life that is full and good." John 10:10b

These last chapters, and the next, show how the thief comes, how we can thwart his attacks through the Word of God, and by standing in the authority we have through Jesus Christ. **Please bookmark these pages as the prayers may come in handy on your journey.**

For today: Allow yourself to soak in John 10:10b, the words spoken by Jesus. ***"But I came to give life—life that is full and good."***

Look at this scripture in other Bible translations to receive other powerful words to expand your mind and revelation.

PRAYER

Father we thank You, that You sent Jesus to die for us and that when He rose again, He gave us life—life abundantly.

In the mighty name of Jesus,

Amen

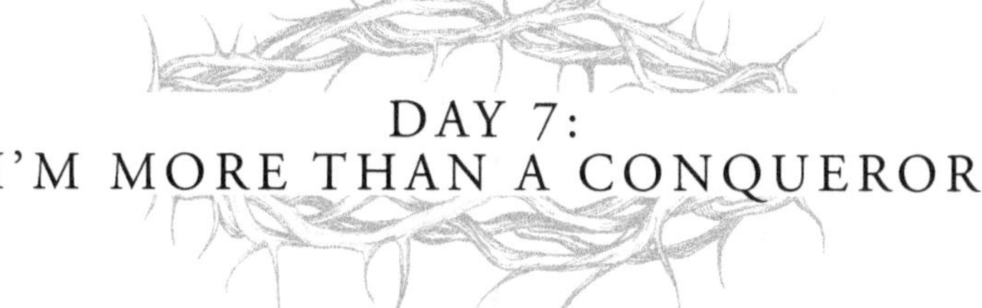

DAY 7:
I'M MORE THAN A CONQUEROR

Yet in all things we are more than conquerors
through Him who loved us.

~Romans 8:37 NKJV

4–7 OCTOBER, 2014

I had been having tormenting dreams. I would wake in the night gasping for air. Sometimes I would wake screaming, crying, or fighting in my sleep.

I dreamt I had spiders and parasites in my body, crawling and attacking me from the inside out. There were centipedes coming out of my eyes, ears and mouth.

During the day, these dreams would plague my mind like a never-ending movie. The pictures in my dreams were very vivid. Then the words, ***"You're going to die...,"*** seemed to get louder in my mind. I looked a mess, and didn't feel like a conqueror walking in the authority and power of Jesus. I even tried to declare out loud the agreements I had made with God, but terrors shook me in the night, and I lacked sleep.

I knew the battle for my mind was at stake, so on the 8th of October, I texted an apostle of our church network named Norm. He is also my spiritual father in the faith. I needed help.

He gave an interpretation of the dream and then said, *"You have this lump in your pancreas, but it will be benign."* He also gave me wise counsel, *"The enemy is throwing everything at you. That is a good sign, because you are a threat to him. You are more than a conqueror, and you will overcome. God is with you and loves you."* These words, along with the prayer that my apostle gave me, helped me to conquer and overcome.

I'd love to share with you the prayer my apostle sent. He advised me to declare it daily till the surgery, and thereafter when I needed it to help me. May these words bless you, and may you encounter the power of the living God as you read them.

A PRAYER FROM APOSTLE NORM

> *Thank You, Jesus, that You tasted death for me—and You became a partaker of my sinful, disease-ridden flesh and blood, in order for me to be a partaker of Your righteous, healthy, blessed flesh and blood.*
>
> *Thank You that as a result, You have blotted out my sin's written against me and nailed them—and my disease—to the cross.*

You have forgiven every cell, fibre and atom of my pancreas. Therefore, every part of it is free from sin and from sin's sting of death and disease.

Thank You Jesus, for fulfilling all the law on my behalf, so that no disease can come upon me because You are the Lord, my doctor.

Thank you Jesus, that my body lives and that it is above the law of sin and death. It lives in the law of the spirit of life in Christ Jesus.

In the mighty name of Jesus,

Amen

DAY 8: FAITH FAMILY
THAT BRINGS DOWN THE ROOF

5 OCTOBER, 2014

Remember the story of the paralyzed man in Luke 5:18-26? His homeboys made a hole in the roof by taking a few tiles out, so they could lower their paralyzed friend to Jesus, for Him to pray and heal him. They couldn't go through the front door because the room was packed out with people!

Well, God blessed me this day with a faith family not only in my church, but from many churches and ministries who stood in the gap for me. They 'brought down the roof' on my behalf so I could be lowered before Jesus to get my healing.

My faith family in my home church fasted and prayed for 21 days that my surgery would go well, that the lump in my pancreas would be benign, and that I would heal and recover quickly. They prayed God's power and love would be on display throughout the entire process, and that the results would astound medical staff. We all need friends and family of the faith prepared to 'bring down the roof' on our behalf, who will do whatever it takes to get us to Jesus for our healing.

In this passage of Luke, Jesus saw these homeboys' faith. He said to the paralyzed man, "Young boy, your sins are forgiven." The paralyzed man was healed.

I believe a huge contribution to my healing came because of the faith of my faith family. They were agents of change for me.

Who is your faith family who can become agents of change on your behalf?

PRAYER

> *Father, we thank You for friendships and the people You surround me with who will bring the roof down for me when I can't. I ask that You would strengthen, empower and pour out more of Your love toward them.*
>
> *In the mighty name of Jesus,*
>
> *Amen*

DAY 9: GIVE THANKS
IN ALL CIRCUMSTANCES

10–12 OCTOBER, 2014

I awoke that morning with an extra spring in my step and a massive smile on my face. I was leaving from Palmerston North for the *Endless Love Women's Conference* being held at our mother church in Gisborne. Thirty four ladies from my church were about to embark on a six-hour journey with no husbands, children, jobs or responsibilities. Yes! Freedom! Just kidding.

I gave up having one of the most important surgeries in my life, to go to this conference. I knew where God wanted me to be: I knew He had something in store for me. However, I was not expecting what I received.

It was the second day, and we finally met our mystery speaker. Her name was Pastor Debbie from Elim Church in Tauranga. She shared one of the most powerful testimonies I needed to hear. Her word was taken from 1 Thessalonians 5:14-18. I love verse 18. **Give thanks in all things.** She told the story of three circumstances and how God taught her the power of being thankful through it.

These three circumstances were: the heartbreak for her mum who fought and overcame breast cancer, the second for her son addicted to legal highs; and the third, she always hid behind her husband.

All these circumstances spoke to me, because they were like mine. When I had received news of pancreatic cancer we were going through teenage trials with our eldest son, 16-years-old, and I was timid, shy, and very introverted—and I hid behind my Hunk, who is tall and very extroverted.

I learnt some powerful keys on the power of praising God and giving Him thanks in all our circumstances. This power breaks the yoke of 'complain-itis' and ungratefulness which leads us to all kinds of things such as resentment, bitterness and even jealousy, if we remain in bondage with it. The more we become thankful, the more freedom we allow Holy Spirit to work in our circumstances. We then position ourselves to witness and become bearers of miracles in our daily lives.

Being thankful is a heart position. We need to posture our hearts and express our gratitude to God and others He uses to help and bless us. When we voice these things, it is a reminder of God's initial intentions from the Garden of Eden—to bless us and to make us a blessing to others.

Even to this day, before I sleep, I give thanks to God for all He has done during my day—and for others he has blessed me with.

I encourage you, every night ask God where He was in your day. Start thanking Him for those moments and miracles, no matter how big or small they were. If you can't think of anything to be grateful for, start with the air you breathe, the hot water you had a shower in, the food you ate, and so on. Before you know it, God will show you more miracles that happened throughout your day.

I'll start you off....

Father, I give You thanks for................................

(In your journal, list things you are grateful for—
or speak them out loud)

In the mighty name of Jesus,

Amen

PS: I can't wait to share with you the encounter with God I had during the *Endless Love Womens' Conference* in Day 10; see you there!

DAY 10: MY ENDLESS LOVE

13 OCTOBER, 2014: EXCERPT FROM MY DIARY

Dear Diary,

I'm home at Palmerston North. I want to let you know of an experience I had during the *Endless Love Womens' Conference* over the weekend. It was during worship on the last night—I wanted to feel the tangible love of Jesus. I reached out to Him and sung to Jesus the rendition of the *Endless Love* duet sung by Luther Vandross and Mariah Carey.

> My love
> There's only You in my life
> The only thing that's right
>
> My first love
> You're every breath I take
> You're every step I make

And I
I want to share
All my love with you
No one else will do

And your eyes (your eyes, your eyes)
They tell me how much you care
Oh, yes
You'll always be…

Before I got to the last line of the song, Jesus appeared and sung the last part:

…My endless love…

Then He kissed my forehead.

When He kissed my forehead, He reminded me that when He died on the cross for me, He took all my sins, transgressions, curses, iniquities and my sickness. I looked into His eyes and I felt an endless love towards me that can never be broken.

I fell to the ground, filled with a deep cry and emotions as I realised just how much Jesus loved me.

I then felt the wings of God embrace me from behind. I felt so loved. It was a love not of this earth, but love that can only come from God, a true 'Endless Love.'

Can you remember your first time you fell in love with Jesus? What about when you felt His tangible love for you? Why not write a reminder to yourself of that moment?

DAY 11:
LONELY, BUT NEVER ALONE

16 OCTOBER, 2014

I arrived at the hospital at 6 p.m., as ordered by my doctor. The time went by so quickly. Before I knew, it was 10 p.m. My Hunk, our children and family that came to settle me into my room on the ward had to leave me. Hospital policies! It was one of the hardest moments being left on my own, and it was not the last time I would experience this. Feelings of loneliness and isolation crept in, especially at nights, as the road to recovery took years.

There are many stories in the Bible where many great men and women of God felt lonely. Elijah was in a state of great distress as he thought he was alone serving God (1 Kings 19:10); King David waited in silence for God (Psalms 62).

What about Jesus? He was abandoned (Mark 14:50). What about Peter who denied Jesus, not just once—but three times (John 18:15-18; 25-27), and Judas who also betrayed Jesus (Matthew 26:47-50)? Jesus suffered alone in the Garden of Gethsemane (Matthew 26:36-46) and was forsaken by the Father when He hung on the cross (Matthew 27:46).

I knew from the scriptures I was never alone, that God, Jesus and Holy Spirit were always with me. I've had many amazing encounters, but I needed an unshakable revelation so that when feelings of loneliness came upon me, I could rebuke it in Jesus name. It took quite some time before I caught this revelation, and still to this day I have to appropriate this truth in my life, especially when feelings of loneliness rise. The difference now, however, is that it's in my spiritual DNA, so I know how to access and activate this truth in my life.

I decided at the end of each day, I would examine how my day was, and invite Holy Spirit to reveal where God, Jesus, Holy Spirit, and the angels were in my day with me. I continue this process today. This helps me to turn my heart to Jesus before I go to sleep, giving Him my worries and cares, then offering thanksgiving to Him. This positions me to receive messages from God in the night.

Why not try this tonight for yourself? In your prayers, ask Holy Spirit to reveal where God, Jesus, and He, were in your day. You may even see your angels at work! Allow yourself to flow with the first thing that pops up from your day. It may surprise you where this thought will lead you.

PRInterfaceAYER

Father, Your Word says You will never leave me nor forsake me, that You are with me always. From today, I choose to look for signs of You and to see You throughout my day, because I know I need you. Apart from You, I cannot do anything.

In the mighty name of Jesus,

Amen

DAY 12: LET IT GO

17 OCTOBER, 2014: PART 1 OF 3

EXCERPT FROM MY DIARY

'Happy 2nd birthday to my beautiful daughter Anahera. Today I choose to celebrate with all the heavenly hosts that this is the day you were gifted to the world to bring God's love to His people. You are as your name says. You are an Angel.

You are my angel walking on this earth, whom I delight in so much.

As I head into having my major surgery today, I am reminded of your birthday celebration we had two days ago, and the theme of *Frozen's* song sung by Elsa, *Let It Go*. It was playing on replay, whilst I was watching you in your beautiful blue dress, your crown, and your beautiful jewellery; not to mention those sparkly shoes you wore—all the while spinning around like a ballerina. Such joy you bring to me as I remember your beautiful day. Anahera, I love you. I'm so blessed to be your mum.'

The nurse came in and said, "The orderlies are on their way to take you down to theatre." I felt fear trying to rise in me because of the unknown, and uncertainty of what would happen.

I then heard a voice say, *"Chontae, breathe. Let it go."*

I looked at my family to see if they had spoken to me, and none had. So I knew it was Jesus speaking to me.

I closed my eyes, took a deep breath in and out. I did this three times.

"Cast all your cares and worries on me," Jesus added.

I took a moment to do that, and then opened my eyes. The memory of Anahera in her beautiful blue dress spinning around came back to my mind, and I was back into a place of joy and peace. Thank you Jesus.

Dear Believer, sometimes we have to contend for our joy and peace. Don't give it away so freely, because it is our strength in God. God says in His Word that joy is our strength, and that He gives peace. These are weapons given by God to thwart the enemy's plans that come against us.

Are there things that you need to let go today? Maybe it's anxiety regarding your surgery, the unknown, 'the what ifs? Whatever they are today, picture Jesus in front of you, and give them to Him. Then picture Jesus giving you something in return.

Remember, Jesus gives us an upgrade. We see that in Isaiah 61, where He gives beauty for ashes, the oil of joy for mourning, and more.

PRAYER

Father, I recognise there are things in my life I need to let go. I invite Holy Spirit to show me what those things are.

(Pause: allow Holy Spirit to show you)

Jesus, today I hand to You...................................

(State the feeling or things you saw)

What would You give me in return?

(Wait and see what He gives you)

Thank you, Jesus, for Your gifts You gave to me. I receive them in Your precious name, Jesus.

Amen

I CANCEL YOU

42

DAY 13:
THE ORCHESTRATOR

Dear Believer,

I want to share something with you that changed my day. I call this day, 'The Orchestrator.'

I'm lying in my bed in the waiting room of the theatre room. It's filled with eight beds, but there is only myself and one other person waiting to go in for our surgeries.

I meet the team who will operate on me: my doctor, his junior doctors, the nurses, the anaesthetics team and medical students training to become doctors. I meet about thirteen different people, all looking at me whilst surrounding my bed. After our initial meet and greet, my senior doctor leaves with a few staff. As he leaves, I overhear the conversation of a male junior doctor speaking to a medical student. He says to her, "This case is unbelievable. I know she (pointing to me) believes in a higher being as it says on her forms, and she is a pastor. Well, this being is looking out for her," he said.

The medical student says, "Why is that?"

The male junior doctor continues: "When she was first referred to the hospital, she came for a scan to look at her kidneys, which only looked at the lower half. That scan was normal. However another doctor from a different department was going past her scan, and saw that there was something higher up that needed to be looked at because he could see an abnormality. So the medical staff here rung her to come back that same day so they could take a scan of her upper body. That is when the doctor found the lump in her pancreas. Someone is watching over her from above!"

The junior doctor turned to me, knowing I was listening, and said, "But you already know this, don't you?"

"I serve a God who loves me, as He does you both," I stated.

The junior doctor smiled at me.

Here's the thing, I didn't know the story the junior doctor was telling the medical student. Hearing him tell that part of my journey gave me the confidence I needed to hear before going into my surgery. What the devil tried to use against me, God smashed and orchestrated a counter-attack against him and his works.

Know this: God is the orchestrator of your life if you allow Him to be. He knows the plans for us, and they are for our good. Any situation that is not good, God can use for our good, if we give Him permission to, and trust in Him.

Use these 5 steps to go deeper in God's Word:

1. Pray
2. Read
3. Meditate
4. Apply
5. Pray; using the two scriptures below

"And we know that God causes all things to work together for good to those who love God, to those who are called according to His purpose" (Romans 8:28).

"For I know the plans I have for you," declares the Lord, "plans to prosper you and not harm you, plans to give you a hope and future" (Jeremiah 29:11).

PRAYER

Father, I thank You that You are the orchestrator, the author and perfecter of my life. Today I choose to line up with every good plan and purpose You have for me.

Where circumstances in my life feel like a storm, I choose to remember that You will cause everything to work together for my good according to Your purpose to bring me prosperity, a hope and a future in Jesus' mighty name,

Amen

I CANCEL YOU

DAY 14:
SCREAMING CHILD

"Chontae," I felt a hand on my shoulder. "Chontae, I'm just going to flash a light in your eyes," said the nurse.

Still feeling drugged from the anaesthetics, dazed, and not knowing where I was, the nurse said, "Your operation is done. You are now in the waiting room of the theatre. I'm just going to flash the light in your eyes to check you, Sweetie." My memory came back. I remembered I was in the hospital.

I felt immense pain in my chest, and I couldn't breathe. I was struggling to find air, and what made it even more excruciating was the pain where they cut me open. I was in agony. The nurse was amazing. She saw I needed help and put an oxygen breathing mask on me. She asked if I had any pain. I nodded.

A little while afterwards, the doctors did an x-ray on my lungs. As this was happening, a little boy screamed. He was in so much pain. He got louder and louder as things got worse for him. He sounded just how I was feeling. Medical staff couldn't calm this little boy down.

I reached out my hand towards his bed and prayed for him. I prayed the Kingdom of God would come and invade the atmosphere with peace, that this little boy would feel comfort, that the love and healing power of Jesus would saturate him.

The boy began to settle, but was still weeping because he wanted his mummy. Then I heard a woman's voice, "Mummy's here. It's ok." The boy became calm. Thank goodness!

I share this story, because in our deepest agony and pain, there's always someone worse than we are. As kingdom carriers, we have the authority and power to bring heaven to earth; to change atmospheres bringing, peace, love, joy, healing, laughter and goodness—all the things that come from heaven and are needed to transform our earth.

PRAYER

> *Father, thank You that I am a kingdom carrier who brings heaven here to earth. As a kingdom carrier, You have given me the power and authority to bring change here on earth. In Jesus' mighty name,*
>
> *Amen*

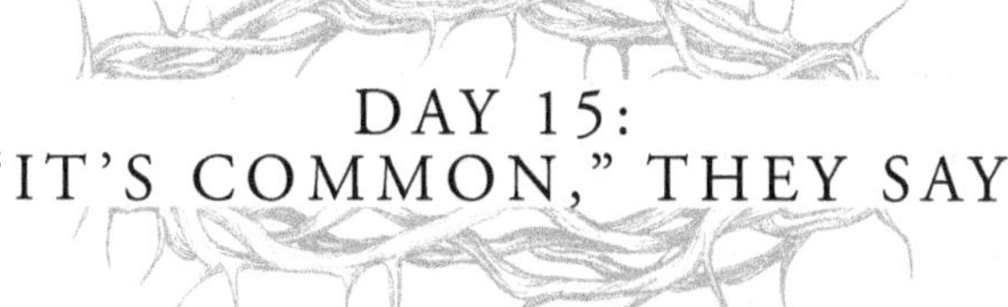

DAY 15:
"IT'S COMMON," THEY SAY

21 OCTOBER, 2014: EXCERPT FROM MY DIARY

Dear Diary,

It has been four days since my operation. I'm told everything went well, and guess what—the operation took six hours. They found the lump and cut it out. It was bigger than a golf ball in size, and looked aggressive. I'm unsure what 'aggressive' means, but they got it and were able to extract it all. They also took half my pancreas, my lymph nodes, and my spleen out.

I'm told that having half a pancreas means I'm more prone to diabetes, as the pancreas produces insulin for our bodies. It also helps our digestion system. Having no spleen means I have no immune system, and taking out a few of the lymph nodes that carried a few of the cancerous cells would prevent further spreading.

I have lots of tubes coming out from my body, 22 staples running down my stomach, beginning from just under my breast, all the way down past my belly button. The great thing is, if I have a long term scar left behind, it will just look like the other stretch marks I have from child bearing. A bigger celebration is I have lost weight. Yeah, winning!

There have been a few *boo hoo* moments, and I can't have a decent shower yet. I still have to have a sponge bath. Do you know how horrible this feels? Not to mention having all this dye from the operation, and dried blood everywhere, and lying in bed for days not having moved yet. I feel sticky and smelly. I could use a shower.

I have had a few setbacks: a collapsed lung which developed pneumonia, and heart murmurs. They think I may have had a minor heart attack, so I'm waiting on more tests.

God, thank You for those who made morphine. Bless them because I'm in so much pain. I'm even more glad I can administer it to myself. Yes! I press that button like its a video game. God, I know my healing is on its way, but while I'm waiting, thanks for the morphine. Top man!

PS: I'm overhearing doctors and nurses saying it's common to have all these setbacks after a major surgery. I'm like, 'COMMON'! I tell myself, "No, sorry. I don't come into an agreement with that, because in Heaven these types of sickness and setbacks are *not common.*

*"Body, listen to me now. You are healed—and the things happening in your body are not common in Heaven. You hear me. **I cancel these setbacks. God let your Kingdom come, Your will be done in my body right now.** In Jesus' name. Amen."*

I'm getting tired now, might be the morphine and my writing is turning into scribbles. I can't even read it. Diary, I'll talk soon.

Question: What are **your** revelations about the setbacks you've had on **your** journey? Do you consider them normal or common? Once you have decided, ask God what He thinks about them, and write the answer in your journal.

52

DAY 16: KISS GONE WRONG!

WARNING! THIS CHAPTER IS A LITTLE GRAPHIC

Have you ever kissed the water of the toilet bowl? Of course you haven't, and nobody plans to. It's not the prettiest thing to do, nor the healthiest thing to kiss in the world. I could think of one thing that is better, and no, it's not a frog that turns into a handsome prince, but it's my handsome Hunk (hehe).

I had been up all night. I was having side effects from the millions of medications. All right, that's an exaggeration. It was only 15 medicines morning and night, and lots of pain relief during the day—but it felt like a million.

These medicines made me feel like I was on a rocking boat with sea sickness. I was also running a fever because of the infection I was fighting, and on top of that, I was still overcoming pneumonia. I spent the night close to the toilet bowl. Ever tried to vomit when there is nothing in your stomach? Convulsions, over a long time, are very painful. As I continued vomiting, there was a period when I had my head down the toilet bowl. The only thing I knew to do in these extreme trials was to appropriate the Word of God in my circumstance. It had helped me when I gave birth to my children. I knew it would give me strength and peace during the storm I was encountering now.

"You, Lord give me strength, when I am weary, You increase the power of the weak." —Chontae's version of Isaiah 40:29. I fell into a deep meditation, visualising God giving me healing power in my weakness. I saw two muscled arms, showing me God's strength and power was with me. I then felt my head lowering, going deeper into the toilet bowl, and I ended up kissing the water in the toilet. Lucky for me, it wasn't a lot. As I said before, not the prettiest thing to kiss.

I share this part of my journey because the road ahead can be a long one, filled with moments like mine. Kissing the water in the toilet bowl is not fun, and neither are convulsions, fevers or pneumonia. It may feel like the days are getting longer, and there are questions like, *'When will this end?'* When will You heal me, O Lord? That last question especially, can arise often on your journey, and it did for me. We will talk about this question in another chapter.

For today, meditate on Isaiah 40:29: *'He gives strength to the weary and increases the power of the weak.'*

Wow! God gives strength to those who are weary, and increases the power of the weak.

PRAYER

Father, you are the GREAT I AM, almighty, and powerful. I loose Your power that works in me, to rise in Jesus' name. When I am weak and weary, Your Word says You increase power to overcome. Have Your way in me.

In the mighty name of Jesus,

Amen

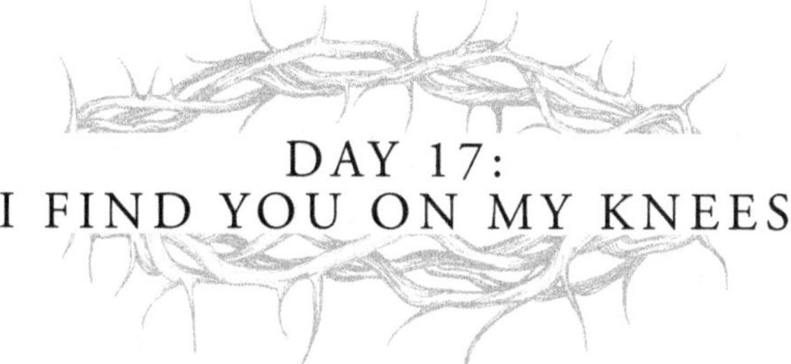

DAY 17:
I FIND YOU ON MY KNEES

24 OCTOBER, 2014

After a sleepless night, sore stomach from all the convulsing, and still feeling a little drugged up, I closed my curtains all day so that my bedside buddies wouldn't talk to me.

This was the first day I'd felt down about everything and wanted to just roll over into a pit of darkness. I wanted to close my eyes and hope everything I had gone through was just a bad dream.

I had a pity party with myself as I replayed the few weeks leading me to this point. Huge surgery, pneumonia, infections, vomiting, pain and agony from where they cut me open, a minor heart attack, having to teach myself how to walk and sit again, and unable to eat my food as my digestive system was not working! I wanted McDonalds. A nice Kiwiburger would have been fantastic right about then. And what about all those medications? Above all, I missed my Hunk and children. I longed to go home, but knew I couldn't.

I heard a soft voice, say; "Chontae, are you ok, dear?"

Thank goodness, it was a heavenly voice from my room buddy Dawn, an 82-year-old lady. She snapped me out of my misery.

I replied, "Yes, I'm ok. I had a rough night. I'm just needing lots of rest, thanks Dawn."

"All right, let me know if I can get you anything, dear."

"I will, thank you Dawn," I replied.

I decided I needed to get out of this pity party in my head. I needed to bail out all the negative 'friends' that were in the boat with me. I put on Kari Jobe's album, *Where I Find You*, and played the song, *'I Find You On My Knees.'* I needed a song that told how I was feeling, yet one so anointed that it would break the yoke, chains and bondage I was experiencing. I needed something that would turn my heart toward Jesus. I hadn't heard this song before. I allowed the lyrics to permeate into my being, and then a picture came into my mind of myself kneeling before Jesus, offloading all my burdens onto Him. I felt myself with a tremendous heartache. I felt all the frustration and pain, I was vulnerable.

For the first time through this journey, my emotions were unstable. I tried to hold it in, but I could no longer do it. I let out one of the deepest cries, as if someone had just died. And something had died. It was part of me. I found I was mourning the removal of two organs that had been a part of me. I discovered how traumatised my body felt.

I rolled to one side facing the window. I wiped my eyes, and felt my eyelids getting tired. As I was falling asleep, I noticed the shift in the atmosphere. I knew, I wasn't alone. I felt the presence of one of my angels beside me. He touched my head, and I fell into a deep sleep.

Have you ever felt or seen an angelic presence before? Have you ever realised that you were not alone? If you haven't, do you want to? The Bible says, 'Ask, and you shall receive.' Ask God to open your senses to the angelic realm, to take the shutters off your eyes so you will see. Remember, faith is being sure of the things we do not see. Expect the unexpected.

If you have seen your angel, why not write about it, or draw your angel in your journal?

PRAYER

> *Father, I thank You for the angelic realm. I thank You that You have assigned guardian angels to me. I ask that You would unblock anything that would hinder me seeing, sensing or hearing my guardian angels on a day-to-day basis. Father, I repent if I haven't taken notice of their existence. They are heavenly creatures made by You. I ask Holy Spirit to help me become more sensitive to knowing when my guardian angel is in my presence.*
>
> *In the mighty name of Jesus,*
> *Amen*

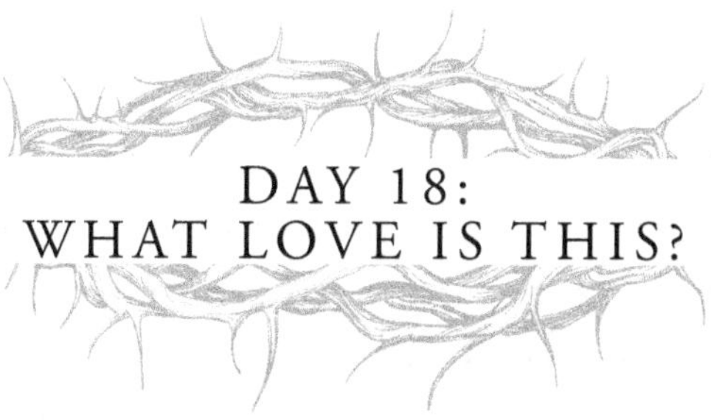

DAY 18:
WHAT LOVE IS THIS?

Jesus in your suffering You were reaching Your thought of me
Jesus in Your suffering You were reaching Your thought of me
What love is this, that You gave Your life for me
And made a way for me to know You
And I confess, You're always enough for me
You're all I need

~Lyrics by Kari Jobe, What Love Is This?

The next few days left me feeling down and exhausted from the previous days of overcoming. I was lethargic and felt like something was pushing me down, like weights had been placed upon my battered body. I could also smell a horrid lingering stench around me. It smelt like death. I'd never smelt death before, but if death had a smell, this was it. What made matters worse, when I looked out my window, the clouds were dark grey and it was always raining, not to mention the wind blowing hard out, blowing the trees from side to side. The weather looked how I was feeling.

I played another song from Kari Jobe, *What Love is This?* It's one of the most beautiful songs I have ever heard. As I continued to look out the window, I saw a bright light beam through the grey clouds. It was as if the heavens opened, and it was the most beautiful light I had ever seen. It was as though two worlds were colliding at that moment. Then I saw a figure walk through the light. I rubbed my eyes as I thought, '*Oh my goodness. I'm losing my mind.*'

As my eyes refocused, the figure was still there. I noticed it was a man, and He was walking toward me. As He got closer to me I knew who it was—Jesus! I knew He wasn't coming to take me home to heaven just then. I was even too unwell to be excited he was visiting me. It was as if the picture paralysed me.

Jesus came closer, until He was standing outside the window. He said to me, **"Have communion with Me."**

I replied, "Come in. It's cold outside." He laughed at me. I realised he was laughing because he didn't feel the cold, rain or wind.

Jesus looked into my eyes and said again, **"Have communion with Me."**

As my eyes met deeply with His, He showed me a vision of Him on the cross, and that He had nailed all my sicknesses, diseases, curses, sins, transgressions and iniquities onto it. He showed me when He looked up at God, and before He spoke the words, **"It is finished,"** that He thought of every human being on the earth past, present and future. Jesus then slowed the picture right down and paused it to what He wanted me to see. The vision was of me.

I burst out in tears as I realised He thought of me—and when He said, it was finished, *He meant it.*

Jesus reached out to my face and wiped my tears away. Love, warmth and joy comforted me, and for a moment, I felt no pain. I no longer felt I was of this world, but part of the Kingdom of God. I looked up at Him, and He said again, **"Have communion with Me."** Then He turned away from my bedside, walked through the wall, out the window, and back into the grey clouds.

I was left hearing the echo of His words, **"Have communion with Me."**

So I messaged my sisterhood and asked them to come and share the word, to worship and pray, but most of all—have communion with me. And they did.

Dear Believer, Jesus loves you with an everlasting love. He thought of you when He looked to God and said, **"It is finished,"** whilst on that rugged cross. When he died, he nailed your disease, sin, curses, transgression, and iniquities to the cross, and wiped them out. He then rose again, conquering the grave, releasing power that you and I can walk in as children of God.

And that's the truth!

PRAYER

Father, I thank You that when Jesus defeated the grave, He gave me life, and life abundantly. I thank You that through His blood, I am healed. I choose to walk in that, in the mighty name of Jesus.

Amen

DAY 19: WHO'S HOLDING YOUR ARMS UP?

> So it came about when Moses held his hand up, that Israel prevailed, and when he let his hand down, Amalek prevailed. Eventually, Moses became weary, and so Aaron and Hur responded by holding up his arms until the Israelites were able to finally defeat the Amalekites. Exodus 17:11

After texting my sisterhood about coming to have communion with me, the majority of them were able to make it on short notice. Someone brought a fresh loaf of bread and someone else brought the communion cups and grape juice.

There was no set schedule, just the Holy Spirit guiding. Whoever had the word, the praise and worship or prayer, was given freedom to lead us. I love these moments of free worship. Holy Spirit had His way, and supernatural power is released in the atmosphere when we take our hands off and let Him do what He wants to do.

I shared with the sisters how hard the last few days had been and why I called them in. Although I was feeling much better, I needed them to help raise my head and arms to the Lord because of the struggles, and I wanted to have communion together. I didn't share my encounter with Jesus with them that day as I felt it was too sacred at that point, and I knew Jesus would let me share when the time was right. As the sisters shared a word about communion scriptures they had received to encourage and uplift me, or prophetic declarations, the smell of death got stronger. My mum leaned over to whisper in my ear, *"Can you smell that?"*

"Yes," I replied. My sisters prayed for Heaven to come and enter our atmosphere and a powerful presence came.

Then one nanny in the church said, ***"Death, I speak to you and rebuke you in the name of Jesus. Get out right now!"***

As soon as she said that, the smell went. There was a massive shift in the atmosphere, and God's presence was thick in the room.

We took communion together and finished with praise and worship. When had we finished, a family member from the next room walked passed and said that what they heard was beautiful.

I'm so blessed that I had my 'Aaron and Hur' who would raise my hands in the battle, to win the war for me, just like what had happened to Moses. I could not have made this journey alone.

QUESTIONS

Who are your Aarons and Hurs? Who's holding your arms up when you can't? These people will become significant in your journey. Love and bless them—and please take good care of their help. By that I mean, allow them to take care of you even though you may not want them to. Pride needs to die in these circumstances.

Write their names down in your journal, and beside each name write why you are grateful for that person. Maybe write a thank you note to them, and tell them how much you appreciate having them in your life. Pray for them and bless them with a double portion.

PRAYER

> *Father, thank you for the 'Aaron and Hur' that have been called to raise my hands up to You in this battle when I can't. Thank You that You have sent them to help carry my burdens here on earth, although Jesus is the ultimate burden bearer. If I have pride in me regarding their help, "Pride, I speak to you to humble yourself in the name of Jesus. Holy Spirit help me see that they are looking after me. Let me see this as a blessing, not only for me, but them as well. Father, I bless my 'Aaron and Hur' with a double portion of Your blessing."*
>
> *In Jesus mighty name,*
>
> *Amen*

DAY 20:
BEAR WITH EACH OTHER

...and forgive one another, if any of you has a grievance against someone. Forgive as the Lord forgave you. Colossians 3:13

I am so blessed to be the wife of Aaron and mother to our children. If God sent me here on earth to do these two things only, I would be the most blessed person in the entire world. The love that I have for my family and what I would do for them I know is a love only God can give. I'm grateful.

I've been married to my Hunk for 20 years. We have had seven children. Raising a large family has been no 'walk in the park', let alone working on our marriage. Sometimes the struggle seems unbearable.

When the news of the pancreatic cancer came, we began the journey ahead with God leading us through the gate victoriously, knowing that everything would work for our good. What Hunk and I didn't count on was the strain and stress it would bring on our marriage over long periods, and how it would affect our parenting and home life.

In the first year of my journey, our marriage was tested. We had many small arguments. I like to call these 'intense fellowship'. We would exchange harsh words, Hunk and I, even while I was ill in hospital—and especially in the first month after the surgery, because it was so stressful for both of us. Hunk became a full-time butcher, full-time Pastor of our church, and now had daddy-day-care duties required of him as he was covering for me. Hunk was usually the breadwinner—the sole income provider while I was home with our children. He was also taking care of the day-to-day running of our church.

I spent fourteen days in hospital after the initial surgery. I went home for one day, then ended up back in hospital because of a pseudocyst that developed. I had to stay in for a further week. For the next two years I was in and out of hospital because of all the setbacks I went through. Praise Jesus, I now only go into hospital twice a year. Remember, I have no spleen which means no immunity, so common colds can turn lethal within days.

Our children went through so much, I wouldn't be surprised if they needed some ministry in the future from the trauma they experienced. These are no ordinary circumstances, but they make way for an extraordinary God to move in our lives, allowing mighty miracles to happen.

One of the greatest lessons our family learnt is our scripture today, Colossians 3:13. It taught us to live a deeper life of forgiveness just as Christ forgave us, imitating what He gave to us when we were saved. We learned to be compassionate, bearing with each other's burdens, being forbearing and not repaying evil with evil. There are just some battles that are not worth entering, especially when there are high levels of stress and key relationships at stake. By choosing to protect each other's heart, by saying, **"I choose you, above being right,"** these circumstances or my opinions are surrendered to become selfless acts of humility that honour the relationship.

One of the best books on relationships that Hunk and I read was, *KYLO: Keep Your Love On,* by Danny Silk, a Senior Pastor of Bethel Church, Redding. He writes;

"I choose you." This is the foundation of true, lasting relationships. It is the foundation for God's relationship with you. As Jesus declared to His disciples, ***"You did not choose Me, but I chose you..."***

Jesus chose you in the most difficult of circumstances. He chose you while you were in sin, while you were His enemy. His side of the relationship with you does not depend upon your choice, but entirely upon His choice. The question is whether or not you will learn to build your relationships with Him and others upon the foundation of your choice."

PRAYER

Father, I am grateful for my immediate family. Today I choose them over my circumstances, opinions and being right. If I have not treated them with love and kindness as you would treat them, I repent of those things and ask for forgiveness. Give me courage to put things right.

Please help me use Your joy as my strength through my trials, even when I do not want to. Help me protect their hearts and have control over myself, my attitudes and responses. May they be of Your kingdom.

In Jesus mighty name,

Amen

DAY 21:
CONSIDER IT ALL JOY

PART 1 OF 2

....my brothers, whenever you face trials
of many kinds, because you know that the
testing of your faith develops perseverance.
Perseverance must finish its work so that you
may be mature and complete, not lacking
anything. James 1:2-4

There are scriptures in the Bible that I really dislike. One of
them is James 1:2-4, telling me to consider it joy when encountering various trials. It builds up my faith and produces perseverance so that I mature, become complete, and lack in nothing.

Persevering through long-term illness is no joy for anybody.
It can be painful. The body can grow weary during the battle
and it can feel like the circumstances are never ending. If I'm
honest, you can get yourself into a dark valley quickly. Believe

me, I know! I have been there. Some of what you read in the last few chapters was only the beginning. Today, I still have to face new health challenges. Remember, I am missing two organs that play a huge part in our bodies. My other internal organs have to make up for that.

I want to share with you a powerful principle that helps me overcome my circumstances so that I operate from the Kingdom of Heaven and bring it into my present circumstances.

James commands us to consider, meaning to weigh up, make our minds up about something, or judge a situation. Also note how we can respond to our circumstances. The choice we should make is to respond with joy. Our attitude is a product of our will, judgments, and how we respond in circumstances. It is a crucial part in bringing either the Kingdom of Heaven or the Kingdom of darkness into our circumstances. Both are accessible to us by the choices we make.

James uses words like 'all joy'. He's asking us to consider, decide, or make our minds up about something by choosing joy—not just some joy, but ALL joy.

Joy in Greek means *chara* or *supreme joy*. It is the highest form of joy there is. Joy is an inner gladness; a deep-seated pleasure. It is a depth of assurance and confidence that ignites a cheerful heart. It is a cheerful heart that leads to cheerful behaviour. Joy is not an experience that comes from favourable circumstances, but is God's gift to a believer. It is an attribute of God's character becoming a powerful weapon for us to imitate and bring to the earth. It is not a joy that says it agrees with the sickness, but is a joy given by God.

I decided before I had my surgery to always be joyful towards others. Do you know how hard that is, especially when you don't want to be joyful? I made sure I was loving and kind to the medical staff who treated me and took good care of me. I would compliment the cleaners for serving me, right through to the staff that came to take my orders for the menu. I even told those that served our meals to thank the chef, for my meals were wonderful. I would not complain about the hospital food.

With every visitor I had, I ensured I was positive, and even when I had down days, I allowed them to look after me. That was hard, considering I was not good at letting others look after me. I always treated my nurses with the utmost respect and gave a double portion of honour to them, blessing them as much as I could through the way I spoke to them. I ensured my attitude towards them was of the Kingdom of Heaven manifesting the fruits of the spirit. Even in the most agonising and excruciating painful times, I was kind, caring and respectful.

Later, this brought favour to me. Staff asked me to pray for them. Some even called me their spiritual mother. I lead a few to the Lord. The chef would ensure my food was amazing and anything extra I wanted that wasn't on the menu, he made sure it was available. If not, an alternative was suggested.

The cleaners took their time to ensure my room and linen were always clean whilst having conversations with me, allowing me to pray and give wise counsel into their personal circumstances. I got to meet some young adults and share Jesus with them, all of whom I invited along to church. I engaged with my room buddies when I shared a bedroom, ensuring I gave them my full attention, and this allowed me to share Jesus and pray with them as well. I wanted to be an agent of change and bring the Kingdom of Heaven into places that are sometimes filled with much sorrow, grief, pain and death. I wanted people to experience the love of Jesus Christ through me.

I don't know where you are at right now in your journey. Maybe you're already perfect and complete in this area. Wow! Praise Jesus for the work He has done in you. I can only imagine what He may have done to get you to that point. For those still on this journey, I encourage you to use the five steps: pray, read, meditate, apply, and pray to go deeper. The gems and mysteries that hide in scripture, especially ones we dislike, can become the most powerful weapons in our lives.

PRAYER

> *Father, thank You for the inspired words given to James, for me to consider Your joy as a strength I have access to. It is a weapon to be used in me and others to change atmospheres, allowing your Kingdom to come here on earth.*
>
> *Today I make the choice to continuously walk with JOY in all my trials that I am facing now, and in the future. Holy Spirit, I give You permission to guide and teach me in this area.*
>
> *In Jesus mighty name,*
>
> *Amen*

DAY 22: PERSEVERANCE MUST FINISH ITS WORK

PART 2 OF 2

....my brothers, whenever you face trials of many kinds, because you **_know_** that the testing of your faith develops perseverance. Perseverance must finish its work so that you may be mature and complete, not lacking anything. James 1:2-4

Can I be real with you? No one likes persevering through hard times, or being tested—let alone struggling with a long term illness in such a way that it builds up their faith and develops perseverance. When you have hit rock bottom in overcoming a body riddled with sickness because it has not yet aligned with the truth of God's Word, I can guarantee you're not thinking, *'Oh, I'm going to persevere so that this trial can finish its work and I become mature and complete, lacking in nothing. And I'll do it joyfully.'* Maybe that is an exaggeration, but consider that thought for a moment. Pause and take a 'selah' moment. Now ask yourself, *"Do I think this way?"*

James gives us a key to this scripture. It's found in one word—'know', or in other translations, 'knowing.' This one word is powerful in understanding this scripture. Look at the above passage of scripture again, I have highlighted this word.

The word *knowing* in Greek is *ginosko*, which means to understand, to perceive properly, to see things the right way.

Here's a great question to ask yourself. ***Am I seeing things the right way?*** Don't worry if you're not right now. It has taken me several times over the years and I'm still being challenged because I realise I'm not always seeing things from God's perspective. I love my spiritual dad, Apostle Norm. Through my journey, he has always challenged my perception of things, especially regarding the healing power of God. He'll say things like, "Let's look at it from God's perspective."

So, how do you learn the right way to persevere through long-term illness? Here are two revelations I have received. They all come from this *knowing,* that James talks about.

Being willing to challenge your mind, means to make a radical mind shift to see from God's perspective. His Will for us is simple. It is *known* in the Lord's prayer; where it says to bring His Kingdom here on earth (Matthew 6:9-10).

I love what Bill Johnson writes in his book, *The Supernatural Power of a Transformed Mind:*

'The will of God is simply this: 'On earth as it is in Heaven.'....When we pray, "Thy kingdom come, thy will be done," we're praying for the King's dominion and will to be realised right here, right now. He wants the reality of Heaven to invade this rebel-torn world, to transform it, to bring it under His headship. What is free to operate in heaven—joy, peace, wisdom, health, wholeness and all the other good promises we read about in the Bible—should be free to operate here on this planet, your home, your church, your business and your school. What is not free to operate there—sickness, disease, spiritual bondage, and sin—should not be free to operate here, period.'

It is not God's will for sickness for you and me. That comes from Satan's kingdom. However, through this trial, God can use it for our good. It can produce a deeper level of faith and intimacy with Him. It brings about a vulnerability causing a desperation in us so we run to Him. It can then position us to see an increase of healing and miracles, whether big or small, if we persevere.

Through perseverance I have witnessed so many healings and miracles in my body and around me, not to mention some amazing encounters with Heaven.

Secondly, my body cannot comprehend the will of God. However, my spirit *knows* (1 Corinthians 2:12; 14).

What I see and understand is this. When our faith is being tested through trials, our spirit knows the truth connecting us to our eternal positioning and rewards (Matthew 5:11-12). As we stand and persevere, this produces endurance in us. It is a steadfastness, a planting of ourselves further in God. Now you may think, *'Well, that scripture in Matthew is talking about being persecuted and slandered by others. What does that have to do with healing?'* When we look back on our scripture in James, he is talking about 'facing trials of many kinds'. Illness, diseases and sicknesses are in that category. God is looking at our character in these circumstances to see if we have matured.

For example, have I treated my cleaner in the hospital with the same respect and honour as a medical professional? Am I treating and serving my husband or wife as God would have me to, no matter the circumstances presented before me? When we have passed that trial, we position ourselves to receive the eternal rewards in Heaven, as mentioned in the passage of Matthew.

What are your revelations from James 1:2-4? What are **your** thoughts about faith being tested through healing? What about perseverance? Is that something **you** are good at?

PRAYER

Father, thank You for trials that come my way. They help build upon my faith, testing it so that I can mature in my walk with You. I pray for more of Your wisdom and knowledge to saturate me so that I'm able to make the right choices through these trials, so that Your work can be made complete in me.

Holy Spirit, help me persevere and endure through these trials so I may see God's power and healing miracles manifest in my life. I need Your help to see from God's perspective, and not my own.

I cancel any assignment where the enemy tries to hinder me, and in Jesus' mighty name I loose Your kingdom over me.

In Jesus name,

Amen

DAY 23: TRIUMPHS, HEALING AND THE LOVE OF FRIENDS

28 OCTOBER, 2014

> Behold, I will bring it health and healing, and I will heal them, and reveal to them the abundance of peace and truth. Jeremiah 33:6

They had moved me into a room with three other lovely ladies who became my beside buddies. This was the second night of me sharing with them. I'm so glad Dawn and I got to be in the same room, as I have grown fond of her.

I was the youngest in our room. The other ladies were all around the age of 80 years. All were still married to their husbands of 50, some 60 years—and had children, grandchildren and great grandchildren. We all were able to meet the other's families as they visited. They shared their lives with me, the great, the good, the bad, and the ugly. I fell in love with the many stories they told. I felt honoured that God would place me in a room full of wisdom, beauty and counsel. I would ask them questions about what it was like in their younger days, their secrets to a great marriage, how they found today's world and so on. It really was enriching. I felt like Titus 2:3-5 had come alive, as if pearls of wisdom were being handed down to me. I loved it.

One day I asked if they believed in God. The ladies opened up that they did, but somewhere in their journey I sensed they had grown cold in their hearts toward God. I could hear the discouragement, disappointment and religiosity. My heart was hurting for these ladies. I asked if I could pray. Thank goodness they were open to it. When I finished praying, I felt the peace and healing power of God enter the room. It was like God entered saying, ***"Behold, I bring you healing and great health. Here is My peace."*** It was as if the passage in Jeremiah 33:6 just came alive.

One lady said, "Thank you. I feel so at peace, and my stomach is not sore any more." The other lady, who hadn't eaten for days, let out this great big fart and we all voiced our joy and celebrated with her by lifting our hands in the air. We even encouraged her to keep going! One nurse came running in to see what all the noise was, and realised we were celebrating farts! Later that day, Dawn reported she had passed bowel motions—at last. We lifted our hands in celebration. And I could finally eat my dinner, having not been able to eat since the operation.

Now you might not think there is anything miraculous or healing about that. But, passing wind (farting), passing number two's, and eating—are signs the body is healing. They are also signs that going home is nearing. This was one of my most favourite memories. I will treasure it for life.

Let me encourage you today. You may sit in your hospital bed staring outside the window, longing to be out in the world in the fresh air, or you may think about the coffee dates you could have with friends, or hope to be surrounded by the love of your family members and get back into your old way of life. Instead, I encourage you to look for opportunities in your ***present*** hospital room to do these things with your bedside buddies—to have a coffee date with your neighbouring patient, to connect with others in your room, sharing experiences and praying for healing. Be sure to celebrate in each other's triumphs and victories, no matter how big or small.

Allow God to invade the space you are in. You have the authority to change any atmosphere and bring the Kingdom of God so that others feel His love and peace and experience His healing power. I can guarantee, there is something about doing for others that brings healing to us as well.

PRAYER

Father, help me seize every opportunity to shine Your light into every situation that I'm put into. Help me bring Your Kingdom here on earth through loving on my neighbour when I am in the hospital listening to their stories. Help me to build a connection with them. Help me see the miracles that are everywhere around me.

Holy Spirit, open my eyes to see where You are at work in my current circumstances.

In Jesus mighty name,

Amen

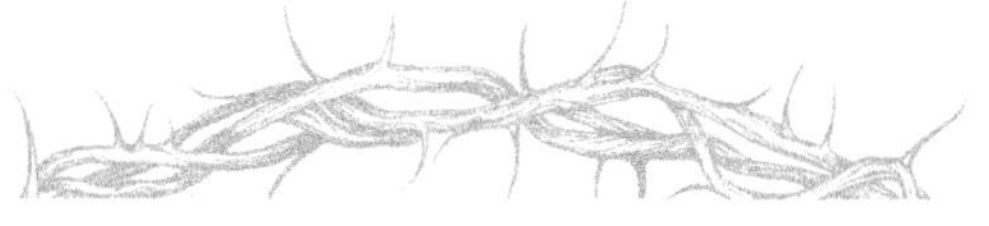

DAY 24: GREATER LOVE

Greater love has no one than this; to lay down
one's life, for one's friend. John 15:13

I dedicate this chapter to all the faithful, loyal, loving, kind and caring friends out there who are supporting their beloved friend who is ill. May the love of God pour out over you, and a double portion of blessing be made unto you.

If I could reward you for your friendship towards your beloved friend, like Heaven will when you get there, I would. But such rewards can only come from the Father when you meet Him one day.

There are no words that can express how much you will mean to your beloved friend as you continue to pray, to sit with them for hours on end in the hospital, when you laugh, cry and share in their journey, when you lay your life down for them. I believe it takes a brave person like you, who has the love of God from Heaven oozing through them to do that. The world is a better place because you are in it, bringing God's kingdom and touching the lives of many people. We need more friends like you in this world.

Dear Believer, I have such a friend, well, a few to be honest. This special friend whom God placed on my journey will remain in my heart forever. Her name is Maiaa.

I want to tell you about Maiaa because she is so special. Such a true godly friend is scarce these days.

Maiaa had been in our church for a few years. She was also on our leadership team under our previous pastor, but I had not really known her well. Her husband is Greg, and they had four children then. Now their family has grown to five children.

When Maiaa came to visit me at the hospital, she stayed for hours talking to me. I felt I connected to her on a spiritual level. It was like I'd always known her, and that we had been friends forever. We could talk about God, marriage, children, our past, revelations, and much more. Before we knew it, it was 9 p.m. at night and the visiting hours were over. Maiaa would then go home, but say she would be back to visit again.

After Maiaa left, I thanked God for bringing her. I had tears of joy as my heart felt so filled with love. The deep longing to find such a friend had been with me since I was a child. God was answering my prayer. Two days after her first visit, Maiaa returned just before dinner time. Before we knew it, it was 10:15 p.m., and she had to leave again. This became a good habit in a bad situation. Every time I was in hospital, she came.

Maiaa is like Jonathan in the Bible. She would lay her life down for me; she would even take the clothes off her back for me. She would be my Aaron and Hur, raising both my arms to God when I've been very low. She would be my cupbearer, armour bearer, and any other *bearer* that there is!

Maiaa celebrates in my victories and is a friend that stays with you in valleys without saying anything. Just her presence was more than enough. I could ring her and cry if I needed to. She is noble, faithful, and resilient. She is a lioness who has protected me during the years that Hunk and I have pastored the church. She had my back, just like Jonathan protected David from Saul.

In Hebrew, her name means 'close to God'. This is something she walks out in her daily journey. It shows through her love, wisdom, and the power that flows through her, especially when she sings. Oh, she has the voice of an angel with power to bring Heaven down. It breaks any demonic activity that may be lingering.

She is my Maiaa who has blessed me so much. I'm grateful for MY Maiaa. She is a gift to me from God.

Today, let's celebrate our friends by showing our love and gratitude to them. Think about how you can show your gratitude for having them in your life. Perhaps it could be a gift, a special prayer, or a letter written to them, letting them know how much you appreciate them. That may be all that is needed.

PRAYER

Father, thank You for the deep friendships I have on this journey. I am enriched by their love, kindness and caring hearts. I ask that You would bless my friends with a double portion. Help me to do the same, and be the same to my friends. Help me to be a 'Jonathan' to my friends.

In Jesus mighty name,

Amen

DAY 25: I CANCEL YOU

28 OCTOBER, 2014

> He sent out His Word and healed them, He rescued them from the grave. Psalm 107:20 NIV

The doctors did their rounds earlier than usual this morning. The doctor who had done my surgery came. I hadn't seen him since the surgery, so I knew this wasn't a normal check-up visit.

We went through all the normal procedures and checks, which all seemed to go well. The doctor said, "Depending, how you go tonight, you may go home." I thought, **YES!** This is why he's come, to release me and send me home.

However, that wasn't the only reason he came. The doctor continued saying, "We have the results from your surgery." My heart went from gladness to being anxious. Then a thought crossed my mind: *It will be ok'*, and a peace came over me.

The doctor continued, "The results showed the lump—the cyst—was benign. You have someone watching over you from above!"

I screamed the hospital down with a massive, ***"YES, YES, YES!" Praise you, Jesus! By Your stripes I am healed. Take that, pancreatic cancer. You are cancelled! I cancel you, I cancel you, I cancel you in Jesus name!"*** I shouted.

I had known right from the beginning it would be benign, because I wrestled with God about it. Wrestling with God is something I will cover in the next chapter.

As my doctor was leaving, he gave the junior doctors and my nurses instructions for what he wanted for me today and tomorrow to prepare for my return home. The junior doctor that I spoke about in Day 13 stayed with me for a few more seconds and said, "Someone is watching over you, you know. I saw the lump. It was the ugliest thing I have ever seen, and was borderline to becoming cancerous. You are being looked after from above, I believe that." Then he left before I could say anything further.

I immediately rang my husband, my family, my friends, the senior pastors, and all our faith community with the wonderful news.

What promises has God already sent out to you? This could be through a dream or given to you by your pastors, closest friends, or your faith family in your church. Maybe it was an impression from Holy Spirit or from an encounter with an angel? Write your promises down in a big font in your journal.

Go over them, decree and declare them often. There is power in the tongue. The words we declare and decree out loud are powerful. Think about when God spoke the heavens and the earth into creation. You have the same power that lives in you. Start speaking it out!

PRAYER

Father, I thank You for Your Word and words that you have sent out over my life. I thank You that these words bring life and truth. I choose to stand firmly on Your promises for my life.

In Jesus mighty name,

Amen

I CANCEL YOU

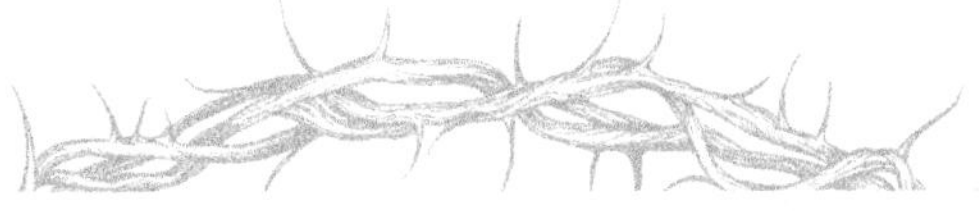

DAY 26: WRESTLING WITH GOD

 READ OR LISTEN TO THE AUDIO BIBLE: GENESIS 32:24-28

Have you wrestled, contended, and never given up until you received your blessing, just like Jacob did?

Sometimes God wants us to be in a position where we won't relent until we have got our healing or blessing. Sometimes, He wants to see how determined we are to chase after Him for it. Why does He do that? It's one of those mysteries that we find the answer to when we go through it.

I remember the first week after finding out the news of pancreatic cancer, a leader in our church gave me the scripture, Genesis 32:24-28. She felt God said I needed to wrestle with Him. So I did. I wrestled with God through my mouth, stating my case, and why He needed me here on the earth, and why I was not ready to come home to Him.

I reminded Him of the plans and purposes He had for my life. I spoke His words back to Him, words He had given me through scripture and prophetic words from leaders. I reminded Him of the dreams He had given me in the night about the things He had called me to do.

I learnt something powerful that day. God already knew everything for my life. He is the author, the orchestrator, the architect, and the finisher. He doesn't need me to remind Him of what He wrote in my Book of Life about me.

I was to wrestle by declaring and decreeing the words God spoke over me, until *I* came into an agreement with the promises, plans and purposes He had for my life. I was determined to fulfill these while I was still here on earth. Sometimes God just wants to see how determined, how hungry for His will we really are.

I wrestled with God for three days and nights, and on the fourth day when the break of dawn came, God confirmed that I would live, through the confirmation of scriptures given to me by one of my senior pastors:

> And may you live to see your children's children (Psalm 128:6);

> This is what the Lord, the God of your father David says, "I have heard your prayer and seen your tears. I will heal you," (2 Kings 20:5).

I knew from that day onwards, the pancreatic cancer would be benign. I also knew that the journey would be a battle, but God would be with me in it.

By now you will have written some promises God has given you. Read them over and over. Wrestle, contend with God, speak to Him about those promises. I did. I held the paper up to Him and said, ***"This is what you promised me. I'm not relenting until You confirm Your promise to me through Your Word."***

Be sure to be specific with God so you know that when He confirms, blesses or heals you, it is from God. Give Him the glory.

PRAYER

Father, today I choose to align myself with every good word and plan that You have written in my book of life. I choose to not relent on those promises You have given me to fulfill here on the earth.

Father, I know Your plans are good for my life. They are prospering me right now. I remind You of why You sent me here, and although You do not need me, I'm blessed and honoured that You choose me anyway. I thank You for choosing me, and I also choose You.

I pray these things in the mighty name of Jesus,

Amen

DAY 27:
GOD, IS IT YOUR WILL TO HEAL ME?

I remember praying many times in the first year of my journey asking that exact question, *"God, is it Your will to heal me?"* Other times I would ask, *"When will You heal me, God?"*

I would read the Bible looking for answers. I would read testimonies of God miraculously healing others. I read healing books one after the other.

To this day, I cannot answer these questions. It is one of those mysteries that we may not understand until we are raised before God and see Him face to face.

What I can say is this. When I read the Word of God and the many healing stories, such as the paralytic lying on the mat being brought to Jesus by the four men (Matthew 9:1-6), the woman with the blood issue (Matthew 9:20-22,) the bread lady whose daughter was healed (Matthew 15:25-28,) the roof friends who lowered their friend through the roof to Jesus (Luke 5:17-39), and scriptures like James 1:2-4 about trials and how to stand through them—I realise God has given us keys to the Kingdom to help us walk through our valleys here on earth.

In all these stories, these people had faith. They were desperate. They had persevered and endured through illness. Above all, they believed that Jesus could heal them.

Throughout my life, God has healed many areas of illness in my body and soul. He has pulled me through the tough times, times I thought would never end. I have seen many miracles and have had so many God encounters on my journey, I cannot express how grateful I am to experience how much God loves me.

Yes, I am still awaiting the other half of my pancreas to grow, ***but have had my spleen miraculously reappear in my body.*** Yes, I have had setbacks that I have had to endure, but I have never given up hope for my healing. Over the years, God has changed my perspective by showing me that healing came in many forms. A few of those ways are through medical practitioners, surgery and medication. Yes, you read that last line correctly!

I believe it's God's idea to have medical practitioners, naturopaths, osteopaths, hospitals, doctors surgeries, nurses and even medication. Why? Because He wants us to be healed. I fought for a year about taking my medication because I thought it was going against God, and that He wouldn't want me to take it. What rubbish, since it was medical practitioners, equipment and the hospital who found the lump in my pancreas. The reality is, I needed all that help and that medication because it helped my healing process until my body was strong again.

I learnt how to pray over my medication, praying that my body would come into agreement with its healing properties. I prayed I would only need it for as long as God intended it, when my body was strong enough without it, or I'd received full healing from God.

Eventually I stopped asking God if it was His will to heal me, or when He would do it, and had a deep-seated revelation that healing is God's will. I am already healed, if not on the earth, it will be in Heaven where there is no sickness. I choose to perceive healing from Heaven's perspective because its perspective is eternal. The Bible tells me in 2 Corinthians 14:16-19, that things of this world are temporal, and I am to set my eyes on the things that are above, that are eternal.

PRAYER

Father, Your will for my life is that I am healed. What is already in Heaven I loose over my life right now in Jesus name. Give me a deep-seated revelation to know that it is Your will to heal me.

Help me grow in my faith and believe in this truth because I need it desperately.

In the mighty name of Jesus,

Amen

102

DAY 28: HE GAVE THEM POWER AND AUTHORITY

In the next few chapters I will try to cover the absolute basics of power and authority. This topic requires a book on its own, to understand it in its entirety. What I write below does not do it justice, but it is a beginning.

> Then He called His twelve disciples together and gave them power and authority over all demons, and to cure diseases. He sent them to preach the kingdom of God and to heal the sick. Luke 9:1-2

Jesus gave the twelve disciples power and authority over all demons, and to cure diseases. He sent them to preach the Kingdom of God, and to heal the sick. Notice in this passage that this was **before** Jesus had died on the cross and rose again after conquering death. This meant they had not yet received the power of the Holy Spirit. After Jesus conquered the grave, He sent us Holy Spirit, therefore releasing further delegated power and authority.

When we gave our hearts to Jesus and accepted Him as our Lord and Saviour, we came under His lordship, and the authority that was given to Him by God is available to every spirit-filled believer and follower of Jesus Christ. Being under this authority enables a believer to operate in the power to bind and loose things on earth, and in Heaven (Matthew 18:18).

I love what Apostle Guillermo Maldonado says in his book, *Power & Authority — To Destroy the Works of the Devil:*

> "Every born-again believer that is under submission to God, and to the delegated authority, can exercise the authority that Christ delegated to the Church against the devil, his demons, his works, sickness, poverty, and everything that affects the territory that God has assigned us. We are all representatives of the law and the government of God."

This is a powerful statement. Those that are submitted to God through Jesus Christ are then given this power and authority. This means you don't have to wait for anybody to pray for your sickness; not your pastor, your husband or wife, or the leaders of your church. You have the same power and authority as Jesus. Here is a key for us to remember: ***Jesus has given this power and authority to you and me, and he also says greater things will you and I do in His name*** (John 14:12, the name of Jesus), (John 16:23).

There is power in the words that come out of our mouth, like a double-edged sword released when we have faith and believe in them.

So let's pray:

Father, according to Your Word, Jesus gave power and authority to cast out demons, cure disease, preach the Kingdom of God and heal the sick (Luke 9:1-2). Jesus also gave authority to trample on serpents, scorpions, and overcome the enemy. This includes all sickness, diseases, curses, iniquities, sins, transgressions and unclean spirits (Luke 10:19), (Matthew 10:11).

*Father, I thank You that the same power that was given to Jesus, who then gave it to the disciples, is the same power and authority that is in me because I am Your disciple. Help me receive a deeper revelation of this truth, a **'greater is He in me'** mentality. Father, I break off any lies that would say otherwise. Lies, I speak to you, and I cancel you and rebuke in you the name of Jesus!*

I am a child of God. I have authority in Jesus name and Holy Spirit power flows through me. Satan do you hear me? I cancel your works operating in, around, and through me. I rebuke them in Jesus' mighty name!

Amen

DAY 29: WHERE DOES THIS POWER ORIGINATE FROM?

For there is no authority except from God, and the authorities that exist are appointed by God. Romans 13:1

God has spoken once, twice I have heard this, that this power belongs to God. Psalm 62:11

In the year 2015, I remember having an open-eye vision into Heaven. I happened to be standing in a house that had many rooms. I was prompted to open the door to a room, and in this room I saw body parts being created. I then walked closer to these body parts as they were in a big pile in the middle of the room. As I walked around it, there were some open sliding doors. Then I saw huge hands come through the roof and down to the pile of body parts. One by one, they were thrown out this sliding door. I had a look to see where they were going. They were being delivered to people on earth.

I seldom have these open-eye visions. In fact, I have only had three in my entire life, and this was one.

I knew those huge hands belonged to God and that He created those body parts to send to the people on the earth who were missing them. I call these 'creative miracles'.

God is the source of all power. He is the creator of the heavens and the earth (Genesis 1). He is the originator, because He has the power to create, exist, speak things into life, the power to bring healing, do creative miracles, and dismantle and destroy the works of Satan. This is a unique power that lives in God.

Satan cannot create. He can only watch God do something powerful, and then try to imitate it. Even then, he is unsuccessful, because what he does is a counterfeit which only brings destruction and evil. This destruction can come in many forms such as illness, lies, and even death. I love what the Online Dictionary says the meaning of counterfeit is:

"Made in exact imitation of something valuable, with the intention to defraud or deceive."

We know Satan comes to rob, kill, and destroy the things that are most valuable to God—which is all of humanity. He is a liar, a thief, a cheat, and can only imitate. Hence, he cannot be God, because he cannot create.

Jesus knew where true power originated from when He instructed his disciples how to pray through the Lord's prayer, when He said to recognise before God that HIS is *the power and the glory for ever* (Matthew 6:13).

God is the 'original' of this creative power. He is the source, because He created all things that come from His glory. All things that God creates are for good, and not evil. (1 Timothy 4:4.)

I believe that God is still creating miracles. Whether there is an organ missing from our bodies, an infection to overcome, a cure needed for lethal diseases, bones growing back, the paralysed being able to walk again, blood clots being dissolved, healing of emotions, a broken heart mended, new medicines being formulated, doctors being in the right place at the right time, and even finances to afford medical bills that are piling up. Whatever it is, God is doing it. God is in the business of creative miracles, because He is the creator from the beginning to the end.

Today, I want you to listen to a song on YouTube. It's called *Create A Miracle* by Luke Braxton. It is one of the most powerful songs I have ever listened to on my journey. This song brought healing to me in so many ways. Luke and Sonja Braxton are worship pastors in House of Breakthrough in Oamaru, and dear friends of mine. Luke wrote this song for his nephew who was conceived with only one kidney. He sang this over his unborn nephew and when the parents went to their next doctor's visit, to the doctor's surprise, the baby now had two kidneys!

Wow! Praise break right now. Hallelujah! Praise you Jesus. Let's pray:

Father, I'm reminded of the words from the 'Waymaker' song'. **"You are the Waymaker, miracle worker, promise keeper, light in the darkness. My God, that is who You are."**

I say have Your way and create a miracle in me. I believe You are the creator as it was in the beginning when You created the heavens and earth. Today, You are the same powerful God, the Great I AM. Yesterday, today and forever, You are the same. God, You have permission to create a miracle in me.

In Jesus' mighty name,

Amen

DAY 30: KEYS THAT HELPED ME ON MY JOURNEY

In this chapter, I want to summarise some keys that helped me on my journey. Some of these are from this book, and some I have not mentioned before. I have read many books, and wished they had a summary or list of things that the person had done throughout their journey, so I didn't have to flick through the many pages to try find the key point I was looking for. I decided when I wrote my own book, I would put a list in it. So here it is:

- I became a watchman over my ear and eye gates to protect me from agreeing with Satan's lies through what I heard or saw.

- I would only allow the Word of God, or positive words to be spoken over my life whilst in hospital. I discussed my wishes with my close family and friends.

- I was careful in what I allowed to enter my mind. Although I didn't achieve this 100% of the time, I was aware of it, and took captive all negative thoughts (2 Corinthians 10:5).

- The Audio Bible is a great application to have. Even when you are in the darkest valleys and cannot read, the audio can read to you. I love the dramatic way the Audio Bible brings the Word to life. Having the different 'voice overs' was incredible. Remember, faith comes by hearing the Word of God.

- Communicate with your, elders, senior pastors and leadership about what is happening. This is crucial, as they will become your prayer warriors on the journey ahead.

- Allow your faith family to be part of your journey, especially those close to you. They want to be there to help you and your family. If they want to pray and fast, and have communion, allow them. Pride has no place throughout this journey. It has to go.

- Write your journey in a diary or journal. This will not only help you and bring healing, but you can go back to those promises from God, and one day, God may have you write a book to help others. I did this, and wrote my book in three weeks. If you would like to know how I did it, please email me at icancelu@gmail.com

- I had a list of praise and worship songs that I would listen to daily. These are great when you are in your valleys. They will help you keep your eyes on Jesus.

- Examine your day each evening to see where God, Jesus, Holy Spirit, and the angelic beings were present that day. There is information about a prayer method I use, called *Examen*. It is on most phone applications, so you can download it to help you get started.

- Have gratitude for your loved ones. Tensions may rise, but only if you allow them to.

- Make agreements with God: Refer to chapters 1 to 3 for further ideas.

- Choose to see things from God's perspective.

- Have a few prayers for spiritual warfare that even make you tremble when you read them out loud. Examples, Days 7 and 31.

- Know who your 'Aaron and Hur' are, so you can call on them to help raise your arms when you can't.

- Wrestle with God for your healing. I didn't stop until I got an answer just like Jacob did. Once I heard from God, I never let go of His promises for me.

- Have a visitor's journal so they can leave you scriptures or positive words of encouragement. I did this because my love language is words. People said they loved this, because there were times they visited and I was asleep. They said it was nice to leave me a message before leaving.

- I used the 5 Steps at the end of this book to going deeper with God, so that I could infuse the Word of God into my mind, body, soul, and spirit. I needed not only knowledge, but revelation that I could apply to my life.

All of the above are suggestions and were a part of my journey that helped build up my faith, perseverance, and endurance. I encountered the healing power of God, and learned how to stand in my authority as a believer in Jesus Christ. These things are a 'must do', and I guarantee they will produce the same outcome for you.

The Lord may also have you do something completely different. This is so amazing, as He knows you more intimately than anyone else ever could. No two journeys are the same, but they enable us to connect to another human being with compassion, empathy, and love towards each other, because we have travelled a similar journey.

PRAYER

> *Father, thank You for Your strategies and plans to help me on this journey. I want to align myself with those things, because they will bring life and healing to me. Thank You for the many creative ways You will do this through me, as they help build my faith and help me to stand in my authority in You.*
>
> *In the mighty name of Jesus,*
>
> *Amen*

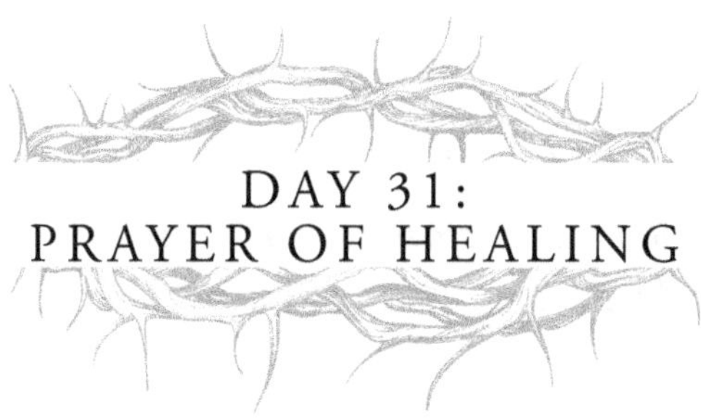

DAY 31:
PRAYER OF HEALING

The prayer in this chapter is not an exact quote but, rather is inspired by the Word of God, and intended to bring the Word into action. It is my prayer of healing that I wrote especially for you!

Beloved, I pray that you would prosper in all things and be in health, just as your soul prospers (3 John 2).

I declare Jesus became the curse for you. He has released you from the curse of the law. You are now the righteousness of God in Christ, free from the curse, free from sickness, disease, poverty and death (Galatians 3:13).

I declare Jesus bore your griefs. He paid the penalty for your sickness and disease and carried it from you. He carried away your sorrows, pain and affliction. Therefore, in Jesus' name you are healed (Matthew 8:17; 1 Peter 2:24).

Lord, I believe in Your promise. It is for my friend who is reading this. It is for their health. Their health has been restored and wounds have been healed (Jeremiah 30:17; Matthew 8:7).

I rebuke the curse of sickness in your body such as those listed in Deuteronomy 28:

Plague 28:21

Tuberculosis 28:22

Fever 28:22

Inflammation 28:22

Tumors 28:27

Haemorrhoids 28:27

Scabs 28:27

Itching 28:27

Mental illness 28:28

Blindness 28:29

All disease 28:29

Boils 28:35

I rebuke the spirit of infirmity in your body in Jesus' mighty name.

I command every organ in your body to function perfectly, the way God intended (Psalm 139:14).

I pray for your immune system to line up with the Word of God and to be strengthened in Jesus' name (Psalm 119:28).

Lord, strengthen my friend and become their song. Lord, You are their salvation (Psalm 118:14).

In times of weakness, be their strength (Isaiah 40:29).

Thank you, Lord, that my friend will live and not die, and will see the generations to come (Psalm 128:6).

Father, I bless Your Holy name. I do not forget Your benefits; You have forgiven all my friend's iniquities, and You have healed their diseases. You have redeemed their life from destruction and have crowned them with loving kindness and tender mercies. You satisfy their mouth with Your goodness, so that their youth is renewed like an eagles (Psalm 103:1-5).

In Jesus' mighty name I pray these things,

Amen

5 STEPS TO GOING DEEPER INTO GOD'S WORD

Here are five steps I have learned to use when reading the Word of God. These steps have helped me in my walk with God. You may have your own walk, so please, by all means use what works for you.

Pray ❧ Read ❧ Meditate ❧ Apply ❧ Pray

PRAY before you read, asking Holy Spirit to illuminate God's Word and help bring understanding. There is no set formula. Remember, this is a conversation with God.

READ the scripture or passage. I like to read it over several times so I get the context and theme. You may also like to read it over several times.

MEDITATE on what you have read. Some days it may be for an hour. It could be for a day, or even a week. I like a passage of scripture to permeate into me. Write your observations in your journal, or questions that come up and verses or words that relate to you. What words 'jumped off the page', or caught your attention?

APPLY what you have you learned from God and from His Word for your life. Think it through. Ask yourself, did this passage of scripture:

- Come with a promise to claim
- An action
- A warning

You may write how you will apply this to your life, using your journal to write your answers down.

PRAY again, asking God to help you live out His word. This time, turn what you have learned into prayers. For some chapters, you may find you have written a declaration which speaks life over you. It may also release the authority that lies within you because of Jesus. These can become powerful weapons in times when needed the most.

GET YOUR FREE
AUDIOBOOK

To get your
FREE COPY
of the
I Cancel You
audiobook
go to

www.chontaetaingahue.com/
i-cancel-you-sign-up-free-audio

Get into your study and receive your kingdom healing
➜ chontaetaingahue.thinkific.com

ABOUT THE
AUTHOR

CHONTAE TAINGAHUE and her husband, Aaron, were the Senior Pastors of the House of Breakthrough Manawatu in Palmerston North, New Zealand for four years. In August 2018, God called them to Gisborne where they are on the pastoral staff at the House of Breakthrough Gisborne Church under Senior Pastors, Norm and Jess McLeod.

Chontae and Aaron have seven children and one granddaughter.

Contact Chontae on
icancelu@gmail.com